# The Flying Dutchman

a new English libretto by

Glyn Maxwell
after Richard Wagner

**First Published in 2023**

by Live Canon Poetry Ltd
www.livecanon.co.uk

© Glyn Maxwell 2023

978-1-909703-33-9

**Cover Artwork: Laura Whitehouse**

live
canon

The Flying Dutchman (2023), based on an original idea by Lucy Bradley, was developed and commissioned by OperaUpClose in partnership with Manchester Camerata

Premiered in June 2023 at Turner Sims, Southampton

Original Touring Production – Cast and Creatives

| | |
|---|---|
| **Starlight** | Philippa Boyle |
| **Captain Dee** | Timothy Dawkins |
| **Helm/Mari** | Carolyn Holt |
| **Mariner** | Pauls Putnins |

| | |
|---|---|
| **Composer/Orchestrator** | Laura Bowler |
| **Associate Orchestrator** | Robin Wallington |
| **Director** | Lucy Bradley |
| **Music Director** | Timothy Burke |
| **Set & Costume Designer** | Ana Inés Jabares-Pita |
| **Lighting Designer** | Neill Brinkworth |

Generously supported by:

*THE FLYING DUTCHMAN* Syndicate

Dominic Collier
Nick and Dee Jones
Julia P Ellis
Jeremy & Alethea Furniss
Chris Greene
Lucinda Jamieson
Peter & Veronica Lofthouse
David MacFarlane
William & Felicity Mather
Nancy Neville
Annmaree O'Keefe
James and Caron Palmer
Gerry Wakelin
Carolyn Ward
John Ward
Garry Watts
Clare Williams

Supported using public funding by
**ARTS COUNCIL**
**ENGLAND**
LOTTERY FUNDED

THE GOLSONCOTT FOUNDATION

The Garrick Charitable Trust

## A note from Glyn Maxwell

Writing this libretto for Opera UpClose's new version of *The Flying Dutchman* is the third time in my life that I've encountered the story. I came across it as a child, in a book of sea mysteries and ghostly tales, and was pleasantly horrified by the thought of a sailor losing a bet with the Devil, being cursed to haunt the sea, trying forever in vain to round the Cape of Good Hope. In my mid-thirties I decided to write it as an epic poem, which became *Time's Fool,* ten thousand lines of *terza rima* inspired by Dante's *Divine Comedy*. For that novel hellscape, I swapped the death-ship for a mysterious empty train. It brings the protagonist to his home town for one night every seven years, as he tries to find the solution that will free him from the curse.

In preparing *Time's Fool* I realised that there *is* no essential source for the legend of the ghost-ship called the *Flying Dutchman*, just various disputed fragments and reports of sightings from shocked sailors across the oceans and the centuries. In some versions all the ghosts are plague-victims, which is why they could never land, in others they are trying to deliver letters from a hundred years ago. The ship's sails are always full though there's no wind; it glows with a ghastly light. In one French telling the spectral ship is so vast it takes years to change its course.

The 'one night in seven years' idea came to Wagner from a Heinrich Heine story, as did the idea that only true love would redeem the Mariner from the curse. I kept the 'one night in seven years', making it a Christmas Eve, but I added the twist that *my* Mariner, or Passenger – a somewhat autobiographical teenager who falls foul of a ghostly stranger – stays *seventeen forever*, as everyone around him ages seven years each time he comes home. And true love is no more the solution to the unearthly bewitching than suicide or murder or desperate flight.

By the time I was commissioned to write this new libretto, I was thirty years older. I put out to sea again with a new Mariner, but I had no appetite for a tale of undying love, or any supernatural intervention. I set this in my contemporary England, a land which, at its borders with the rest of humanity, seems to be putrefying into a realm of fear and cruelty. My first stage-direction sets the story *Here, Soon*. What I conceived of as a dystopian near-future for England feels, after four years of work, along with the delays and calamities of the covid-19 pandemic, more like a contemporary documentary. The monstrous Wave with which the England of this libretto threatens to capsize the boats of women and children fleeing terror was not my idea but emanated from the actual Home Office.

So we have a sailor at the end of his rope, alone and exhausted and hearing voices in his head – which are not ghosts at all but real people in the hold of his boat, his terrified passengers who've paid him to get them to the English coast. That English coast is bristling with fortifications, with an army of citizen-spotters on the white cliffs, ready to call the Border Police and set the Wave in murderous motion. Wagner's Captain Daaland is not the father of the beautiful Senta, but a grasping naval professional only too ready to take the Mariner's money and run. And Senta here is Starlight, the one dreamer among the brainwashed mobile-swiping vigilantes of the Watch. The refugee she dreams of is an idealized victim, yet the man who stumbles ashore is a wretched people-smuggler who has lost his mind. No one sees anything for what it is. Nor do we see them for what they are until they're faced with the arrival of the Other – and the choice of destroying it or saving it. *It* being a desperate stranger. *It* being the soul of a people. You could say this is a political telling. I say artists have the right to pass judgement on their own Here and Now.

*'Oh, is there light up ahead*
*is there God*
*is there good*
*is there you?'*

Glyn Maxwell, London, June 2023

**Glyn Maxwell** is a poet, playwright, librettist and teacher. His poetry books include *The Big Calls, How The Hell Are You, Pluto, Hide Now*, and *The Breakage*, all of which were shortlisted for the Forward or T. S. Eliot Prizes, and *The Nerve*, which won the Geoffrey Faber Memorial Prize. His Selected Poems, *One Thousand Nights and Counting*, was published on both sides of the Atlantic in 2011, and his epic poem *Time's Fool* is in development as a feature-length film with Fox Searchlight.

*On Poetry*, a guidebook for the general reader, was published in 2012. *The Spectator* called it 'a modern classic' and *The Guardian's* Adam Newey described it as 'the best book about poetry I've ever read.' *Drinks With Dead Poets*, a fictional sequel, followed in 2016. Maxwell is working on a philosophical amplification of *On Poetry* titled *Silly Games To Save the World.*

His plays have been staged widely in the UK and the US. His opera libretti include *The Firework Maker's Daughter*, which was nominated for 'Best New Opera' at the Oliviers in 2014, and *Nothing* (both for composer David Bruce) which was nominated for the same prize in the Sky Arts Awards in 2017. He has also written libretti for Elena Langer and Luke Bedford, and for Mozart's *The Magic Flute*. His new version of Wagner's *The Flying Dutchman* premieres in Southampton in the summer of 2023 and will tour several port cities of the UK.

Maxwell has taught at the Universities of Warwick and Essex in the UK, at Columbia, Princeton, NYU, The New School and Amherst College in the USA, and now teaches on the Writing Poetry MA at The Poetry School.

# Characters

**Captain Dee,** captain of a ship that is laying cables to fortify the island against intruders;

**Helm,** the young pilot of the ship;

**The Mariner,** a man alone at sea, so exhausted he has forgotten about the refugees he is carrying below deck;

**Starlight,** a volunteer member of The Watch, who scan the Channel for small boats;

**Mari,** the leader of Starlight's Unit, formerly her lover;

*

**The Sailors** on Dee's cable ship;

**The Watch,** a team of volunteers who scan the Channel for small boats to report to the Border Force;

**The Travellers,** below deck on the Mariner's boat, whom he has forgotten in his delusion

## ACT ONE

*Here and soon.*
*CAPTAIN DEE's ship caught in a violent storm, unable to land on home soil*

SAILORS
Home wish! Hallo ho!
Home wish! Hallo ho!
Hallo ho! Hallo ho! Hallo ho!
Home & here & here we are
& home & here & here we are
Hallo ho! Hallo ho!
Home & here & home & here
& home & here & home & here
& wish! Hallo way! Hallo way!
Hallo ho & ho way!

CAPTAIN DEE
My country! Forty weeks we toil
In your defence we guard your soil
And here is how you pay us now –
Raising the storm to end all storms!
So near to home and far away
Our heaven close but hell to pay!

HELM
Hey, Cap'n D!

CAPTAIN DEE
How goes it, kid, good news?

HELM
Aye, Cap'n D, I think the storm will clear!

CAPTAIN DEE
Do you now. (She thinks the storm will clear...)
To hell! Lights of my town, I spied my home
England my heart, these forty weeks of dreaming!
Damn this infernal storm in a clear blue sky!
Storm after storm, each one laughs at the last one
Storm after storm, black as souls can imagine
Where is home in this darkness?
Wait though. She's right. The kid's a seer.
The clouds are clearing. Look, my star...
Hey, children, so we land at dawn
Now sleep below, dream dreams of home...
Hey, genius, you think the dawn is coming soon?
Don't close your eyes! (She'd miss the Day of Doom...)

*CAPTAIN DEE goes below*

HELM
I've got the Watch! I'm on it, Cap'n D!
He has set me in charge of the rolling sea
Mine angel – See me now!
I have guided us on the homeward way
Mine angel, Lord knows how!
I made a fortress for your dreams
The island is safe for you
I waved away the worst of storms
What more can your darling do?
Oh ho, homeward we go
Close these eyes I see you true

*She dreams of love. A wave hits the ship. HELM checks there's no damage and goes back
to her song*

HELM
I have all of your letters by heart right here
Mine angel, send me more
For I haven't had word since who knows where

Some far and friendless shore
A storm can bring me to my knees
But so can mine angel too

*She drops to one knee for an imaginary Proposal, she has a little box for a ring*

HELM
I sailed a circle round the seas
To bring this – my gift to you
Oh ho, homeward we go

*She falls asleep. The storm rages. A small boat drifts into view, apparently abandoned*

HELM
I made a fortress for your dreams

*She starts up again, but nods off*
*The MARINER's ship drifts into view*

MARINER
The time is gone
And once again I wake here
Alone at sea
Have seven hours or
Seven years gone by?
So I am yours again
Your little curse sends me around in circles
It costs you nothing
To see me sail in hell
Though hell I didn't think so lonely
Can you even see me?
Oh, if you don't know me
Leave me to die!
One final wave, let go of my hand!
And on the white sand set me free

There was a time I thought this life
Mine to dispose of so I tried
But oh, hell is for life and life's a cell —
A suicide's a night of sleep
Or run my ship hard on the rocks?
But no, soon I wake and all is well
I bared my soul that it be taken,
Be murdered, drowned and turned to bone
Draw near me, you will hear no heartbeat
Stand by me, you will stand alone

So now the nightmares of my youth
Were true, are here, I am the proof
The life-in-death, the death-in-life
Story to scare you to the light
But where is light for one awake
Somewhere the dawn can never break?
No life is here! No light can shine!
Gone from Creation, lost in time
Gone from Creation, lost in time

Love, what of love, can I be heard in heaven?
Love of a maiden, life a fairy tale
Night after night I dream of my redemption
Only to wake alone beside my sail

Love, what of love, they swore to love forever
Vow after vow, oh years on years ago
Soul after soul, fair women O fair weather
Gone like the sun, forever gone below

I wake to nothing! Love? Love was not the way
Love has no time for me now time is gone

And in my dreams I hear the voices
The voices, even now they're here
The souls who sailed the ocean with me

Voices rising through the years
Spare me I beg you! Rest in peace!
I have forgotten who you were
Be silent! Who can help you now?
Nobody can till Doomsday come!
Ah heavens, hear my only cry –
Last of the living, let me die!

*The MARINER subsides into his trance. The TRAVELLERS appear from below*

TRAVELLERS
We who you dream of are no dream

*CAPTAIN DEE returns to deck. Seeing the abandoned boat, and HELM half-asleep, he tries to wake her*

HELM *(half asleep)*
Not now, not now…
I made a fortress for your dreams…
The island…

CAPTAIN DEE
'*Not now*'??? When? When we are dead, you fool?
Look there's a boat, look, drifting on the waves

HELM
Oh blimey no, I'm on it, Cap'n D!
Ahoy! Ahoy!

*Silence*

CAPTAIN DEE
It seems they're dead to everything, like you

HELM
Give answer! Can you hear us?

CAPTAIN DEE
No sign. Below, Sharp-Eyes, and sleep some more.

*HELM retires below*

CAPTAIN DEE
Wait! Something – movement?
Seeing things… Delusion!

*He turns and the MARINER is right there, all in black, drenched from the sea, holding a sack*

MARINER *(confused)*
Can I be seen… Is it here…
The hour of Doomsday…
Are you the same as me…

CAPTAIN DEE
What does he say?
Indeed, sir – we are sailors!
Your country?

MARINER
Everywhere

CAPTAIN DEE
*(aside)* Never mind, there's time for that
Poor soul, how did they come and no one saw?
They shouldn't sail here, can't believe they got this far
Through our defences
Soon the Guard will send them back across the ocean
– Say, your boat there
How many souls within her?

MARINER
I sail alone
There are no souls within her

16

When land appears on the horizon
Loud beats a drum far down inside
My heart a stone forever frozen
Bursts into bloom in wild delight
The pain of hope inside the hopeless
Soon to disperse and die once more
The cry of home inside the homeless
Loss with no end in sight of shore
The howl of home inside the homeless
Loss with no end in sight of shore
Are you my death?
I could not prize you more
Are you an angel, demon, holy ghost?
You know a girl, a wife, a witch
A warning? So be it, I shall
Wake up, on this ocean
Beside my sail in solitude, unknown

CAPTAIN DEE
*(aside)* The man's confused
Time must have marred his reason
– My lonely friend, you surely understand
I have no power to let you go ashore
And I must ask you
I must ask you what your boat contains

MARINER
My boat bears what you see, this sack and I
Both deep and lightless, lost to humankind

*He throws the sack to CAPTAIN DEE who looks inside*

MARINER
You see? Only ancient notes that bear
Only faces, circles after circles meaning nothing

CAPTAIN DEE
What? They're zeroes!
They are banknotes, see!
Are they real? They're real...
This is a fortune...

*He watches CAPTAIN DEE gathering the banknotes*

MARINER
Of what? Is this the harbour sought so long?
Pale sand I see – white cliffs beyond –
All that is yours
If you will take me to the shore

CAPTAIN DEE
What did you say now?

MARINER
Will you take me with you?

CAPTAIN DEE
You know that cannot be

MARINER
All that is yours                                    *[the sack and its contents]*

CAPTAIN DEE *(aside)*
What? Is he mad? There are millions in here
I heard that? I can't have, I dreamed it –
So – if I wake – this will all disappear
I'll sleep and I'll dream, I'll believe it...

                                                     MARINER
CAPTAIN DEE                                          Take all there is, all is dark to me
Think now, while the vision is certain
                                                     All I desire is a harbour
And I won't even blink while he speaks

For sure, he'll be gone like a phantom

And it's I alone, I alone who can see him

What? Cap'n Dee? This is mine in real life?

*All this is yours* – so it's mine
In plain English it's mine

So, Cap'n Dee (oh that's me) I'll decide

One, two, three, four, I've decided
I think I've decided

Captain Dee (yes that's me) I've decided
No one saw him

No one else, I saw him alone
No one saw, I saw him alone!

CAPTAIN DEE
Well, stranger, when I say
I cannot take you
I really mean to say
You're welcome, my friend
See, this my home
With open arms awaits you
*My home is your home*
As we say at sea
You are my Guest here
You're one of us in no time
Do we see eye to eye?
I see we do

MARINER
This is my home?

All I have known is the lonely sea

And silence all I remember

If all that I have so enchants him

It's his, fair's fair, let business be done

For he'll pay his half of our bargain

Oh – and set me ashore in the dawn

Oh – and set me ashore in the dawn

Oh – and set me on land in the sun

Oh – and bring me to life in the sun!

19

CAPTAIN DEE
I give you here my word

MARINER
Your word…
What are we waiting for, my friend?

CAPTAIN DEE
Calm sea, old chap, a berth and soon we're home
And then a boat, a special private boat

MARINER
And then the shore…
My feet upon the shore…
Voices inside me, cease your murmur
I sailed alone, alone I'll go
Hope in my heart, my journey over
And *home* the only word I know

CAPTAIN DEE
Your lucky night, my lucky stars
Two blesséd sailors
Struck gold to meet a kindred heart
My friend, let's keep this luck between us
Why share the joy and lose our part?
A wind, a boat in secret, then there's
A path, a safehouse way up high
There he can hide there's some old bed there
I'll kill the lights and wave goodbye
We'll keep this luck between us
Why share the joy and lose our part?
Why share the joy and lose our part?
There he can hide there's some old bed there
I'll kill the lights and wave goodbye
I'll lock the door and wave goodbye

MARINER
Voices inside me, cease your murmur
I sailed alone, alone I'll go

Hope in my heart, my journey over

And *home* the only word I know
Now I can see the light up yonder
There shines the day I thought was lost

The grace and mercy, love and wonder

The dream I dreamed, a life at last

Oh it's as if the time before

20

My friend, let's keep this luck between us
Let's say we keep this thing between us
Why share the joy and lose our part?
Our lucky stars, two blessèd sailors
Struck gold to meet a kindred heart
A wind, a boat in secret, then there's
A path, a safehouse way up high
Yes! My stars are shining in the sky
And mine is not to reason why
No mine is not to reason why

Passed in one night, was nothing more

Oh it's as if the time before
Passed in one night, was nothing more

Hope in my heart, my journey over

And *home* the only word I know
Oh it's as if the time before
Passed in one night, was nothing more
Passed in one night, was nothing more

HELM *(getting the message from shore)*
Sea calm! Sea calm!

SAILORS
Hallo way!

*CAPTAIN DEE stows the MARINER away on the deck, the SAILORS oblivious in their joy*

HELM
We sailed a circle round the seas!

SAILORS
Home wish! Hallo ho!
Hallo ho! Halloho ho yo ho!

CAPTAIN DEE *(to himself)*
Ah me, I sailed a thousand seas
With rogues and fools and who knows who
But now I'll sail to where I please
On my new yacht of gold and blue!
I shall call it *DESTINY…*
Halloo, halloo!
*(to the SAILORS)* Ah children, one last time!

21

SAILORS
He has set me in charge of the rolling sea
Mine angel – See me now!
Hurrah!
I have guided us in on the homeward way
Mine angel, Lord knows how!
Hurrah!
I made a fortress for your dreams
The island is safe for you
I waved away the worst of storms
What more can your darling do?
Oh ho, homeward we go
Homeward homeward home we go
Oh ho, homeward we go ho
Ho ho ho ho ho ho

# ACT TWO

*The WATCH distracted by social media. STARLIGHT watching the sea*

WATCH
See oh see oh see how she loves him
See oh see oh see she said so
See what's new today
Let us see what our friends all say

Win oh win a week in the sunshine
Dream the dream we dream in no time
Swipe our cares away
Let us see what our star signs say

If she knew me she wouldn't have to wait
The world would know
We'd set the date
And he'd love me it's written in the stars
The world would know
That joy was ours
The world would know
That joy was ours...
See...
See oh see oh see oh see
See oh see oh no it's over
Dream a dream the dream you dream
Dream oh no she's found another
Dream the love that stays together
Find the love that lasts forever
Dream the One and only lover
Dream the dream you dream

*MARI comes to check on the WATCH*

23

MARI
Hey dreamers, there's no time for dreaming
You keep your eyes on that horizon!

WATCH
What's there to see? The sea we've seen
And all the world is on this screen!
The whole wide world is on the shining screen!

MARI
So what? You keep your eyes out there!
What's with you, Starlight? Earth to you?

WATCH
See the sea there's nothing sailing
See the sea a fleet's invading

*MARI looks out to sea in horror — it's a prank*

WATCH
Made you look that way!
If they come we will save the day
We the few who view the ocean
Do our duty to the Nation
Watch for friend and foe
When they come you'll be first to know
But who sails now? no sailor even tries
The night is bright
With starry eyes
And those who try they wind up in a cell
So far from home
So close to hell
So far from home…
See…
See the sea oh see the sea
See the sea a fleet's invading!
View the view we few we view

Do our duty to the Nation
Dream a dream and keep our station
Shield the island from invasion
Raise the Wave to save the Nation
Now and ever more!

*MARI looks at STARLIGHT again*

MARI
You close your eyes – you alone it seems –
At least they're rousing from their dreams

WATCH
She never keeps the watch we keep
She'd sooner we were fast asleep
She waits for one who'll never come
The stranger from her *stranger* dream
Ha ha ha ha!

MARI
I see this! Lost in thought again
It is your work to keep the night-watch
But all your thoughts are miles away

STARLIGHT
Oh watch the ocean? Save the Nation?
Save all your flags for Poppy Day
I see a man…

MARI
There's no one there!

WATCH
Ah bless, ah bless, we do declare
More stories of her mystery man

MARI
Who sails the seven seas alone

WATCH
Call him! Ah wait has he a phone?

MARI
Enough delusions in the dark
Eyes! Ocean! Woman do your work!

WATCH
Don't waste your breath!
She's much too good for us
Thinks she's much too good for this
It's true, it's true, too good for you
Aye-aye, it's true, that's what she thinks
She thinks we're watching all night long
To greet invaders with a song
Don't tell! She'll roll out
The welcome mat so all the world can
Dance on that! Ha ha ha ha
Don't tell! Ha ha ha ha
She will! Ha ha ha ha

STARLIGHT
To hell with all your mindless bother
You sound like no one but each other

WATCH *(louder)*
Me oh me there's no one like me
See me if you like me Like me
I'll Like you the same
And remember my username!
She oh she how's she the bright one?
How's she going to meet the right one?
Staring out to sea
For a phantom, a fantasy!

STARLIGHT
Oh, it's that same old tune forever
It's see oh see oh me till kingdom come!
What if my dream is something deeper
Than you can ogle on a phone?

WATCH
Fine! Let's hear…

STARLIGHT
Yes, you can hear me
If you can lift your eyes to see me

MARI
Not this again, there's no one there
The soul you are dreaming of – let him go

STARLIGHT
His tale's a tale of everywhere

MARI
That doesn't mean he's coming here

STARLIGHT
Hear for yourselves, friends in the night
Dream after dream I see him sailing
His soul's in hell and ours stay silent

WATCH
She called us friends

STARLIGHT
Friends of the truth

WATCH
Let's hear this truth

MARI
I've heard enough

*MARI exits*

STARLIGHT
Alone at sea... the rolling sea...
Alone is he... see him oh oh see...

Nobody sees this broken man
Whose hope is lost, who sees no sun
Sweet souls he dreams he meets again
He wakes to find are dead and gone

Oh! and now the wind!
          and the rain, and the rain
Oh! and now the storm!
          and the waves, and the waves
Oh! is there light up ahead is there God
          is there good is there you?

Please see with me
          this desolate soul on the far horizon
Joy, hope was his
          he led a good life, imagine, imagine
Oh! life was his,
          wife and child, house and garden
All love was his,
          now where in the wide world can it be?

Three thousand miles away from here
A kindly boy toils tirelessly
He learns his trade, an engineer
He finds true love, a family

Oh! will peace remain?
    may it stay, let us pray
Oh! has war begun?
    so they say, fly away
Oh! is there light up ahead is there God
    is there good is there you?

Please see with me
    this desolate soul on the far horizon
Joy, hope was his,
    he led a good life, imagine, imagine

STARLIGHT and WATCH
All life was his,
    wife and child, house and garden
All love was his,
    now where in the wide world can it be?

STARLIGHT
O save our souls, they flee from home
They move by night, they hide by day
No names are theirs, no place is home
With all they have they pay their way

Oh! the truck will go!
    it's a ride, get inside
No! where did they go?
    fell behind, never mind
Go! you're alone, you're alive, it's a ride,
    lucky day, lucky you!

WATCH
Oh, where's his wife
    and his little child
        will they be together?

Story so sad
        it has made us cry
                are they lost forever?

STARLIGHT
*He* sails the sea, seeking a haven, a harbour
Cry, cry your tears, it's not a story now for him
It's told for thee, O see him
For thee! O see him!

WATCH
Poor sailor, poor sailor!
Help him!

*MARI comes back*

MARI
Stop this, stop this! Cease!
What is this nonsense?

WATCH
Far, far out there
This poor man sails
He's lost his children!

MARI
It's in her mind, you can't believe it!
In dreams she wastes her days and nights
Do your damn job – do you have eyes?
The ship is in!

STARLIGHT
What ship is in?

MARI
The cable ship!
Your shift is done

WATCH
We'll meet the ship!
The ship is home!

*The WATCH disperse to go down to the shore and meet the cable ship*

MARI
Wait, Starlight, wait
You'll be the end of me
This is our work and every night
This nonsense, oh
I should fire you now!

STARLIGHT
For what? What's wrong?

MARI
Oh Starlight, *why?*
What do you want from me?
You tell these tales and fools will lap them up
We sweep the ocean
You go spreading poison!

STARLIGHT
What's wrong with you?

MARI
Your charming tale
Is treason!

*MARI softens, goes to STARLIGHT*

MARI
Return, return, to where we came from
The nights we knew, our days as one
We dreamed a future, sang the same song
How can our joy so soon be gone?

31

Night after night, you dream this ghost
Out on the ocean, lone and lost
Open your eyes a poor soul speaks
Right here before you one heart breaks
O Starlight
Here's your phantom, here

STARLIGHT
Well, who's the dreamer now?
You are my friend, I know
You always will be
Yet now I feel
The world has called to me
Can you not hear the ocean?
Can you not hear the future?

MARI *(sarcastic)*
Well pardon me

STARLIGHT
I hear it cry

MARI *(sarcastic)*
All praise to you

STARLIGHT
Let me go by

MARI
What will you do?

STARLIGHT
I'll say goodbye

MARI
I'll count to three

STARLIGHT
Let me go by

MARI
I'll count to two

STARLIGHT
I'll say goodbye

MARI
Oh don't mind me!

*MARI softens again, goes to STARLIGHT*

MARI
Return again to where we came from
Truths that we share
Why fight this way?
O hear, my star, my Starlight, my same one
Wash me ashore
On yesterday
Night after night, you dream this ghost
Sailing the ocean, lone and lost
Open your eyes this sailor speaks
Right here before you one heart breaks
O Starlight
Here's your sailor here

STARLIGHT
What? Do you think that I don't love you?
Poor shipwreck, so you've lost your mind
How can you say that I don't love you
When I love all of Humankind?

MARI
How handy! Oh how nice for Humankind
You love us all! That's quite the wedding party!

You've done the seating plan, the invitations?
You love us all, your Humankind

STARLIGHT
I do!

MARI
Oh have we started?
Where's the ring?

STARLIGHT
O no

MARI
Here's where we form a line for love from you?

STARLIGHT
Why can't I love?
Why can't I show compassion?

MARI
Only to dreams though
Sure you do, feel free

STARLIGHT
He's not a dream
He's out there on the ocean
Oh wait – what?
You believe it's love, true love?

MARI
Starlight, you're pale
Love, I am trying to help you

STARLIGHT
Me? Help the sailor
Out on the horizon

MARI
What sailor, Starlight?
I see no one there!

STARLIGHT
You never do
You have food and your bed
Can you not see what's not in front of you?
Still, still they sail
Those souls in fear
Though we would build a wall so high
Please, see with me
How they dream dreams of here
How can a human close his eyes
And blindly build a wall so high?

MARI
So high?
My dream of the cliffs, oh the shore –
I saw it all –
Something is coming here

STARLIGHT
What's a dream to me?

MARI
Starlight, I dreamed of you
A strange dream
I've had that dream before…
Atop the cliffs I stood one morning
The silver sands spread far and wide
There many souls in bliss were walking
The bells were pealing for a bride
The bride was you, and all around you
Bridesmaids – many – clothed in gold –
A figure rose in black beside you
While from the cliffs I waved and called

STARLIGHT
What figure?

MARI
That's the thing you ask?
Not where was I
But who was he?

STARLIGHT
And who was he?

MARI
Well you tell me

STARLIGHT
What man?

MARI
I couldn't see his face
He stood so deathly still beside you
Your gown was lace and spread forever
He moved in front of you to hide you
I saw two hands still clasped together

STARLIGHT
He held my hand?

MARI
A sailor's knot
And since you seem to like my dreams
I heard his voice from faraway

STARLIGHT
His voice?

MARI
'The world will know your names…'

STARLIGHT
I save his soul
He is the one!

MARI
My nightmare
Let morning fall

STARLIGHT
The world knows us
And life begins

MARI
My day is done
The night is all

*MARI exits in despair*

*STARLIGHT wanders along the cliff, looking out to sea. Up ahead she sees a light, a watchman's hut*

STARLIGHT
Yea, life was his
Wife and child, house and garden
All love was his
Now where in the wide world can it – ha!

*She sees the MARINER, exhausted, sleeping with his head on a table. Astonished, she approaches him. CAPTAIN DEE is sitting in the shadows, he has the sack with him. He no longer wears his Captain's cap*

CAPTAIN DEE
My friend, I ask you not to wake him
Look, he's exhausted
He's a shell
If he is found he will be taken
Believe me
This we both know well

STARLIGHT
He's one of them?
Can it be true?
He's from the ocean?

*CAPTAIN DEE gestures for her to sit down*

CAPTAIN DEE
Please, my friend…

*STARLIGHT sits*

CAPTAIN DEE
Here, you and I, two noble guardians of this island
Why would we let this stranger steal upon our shore?
Long I have sailed and served to fortify my homeland
Tonight I saw a light I've never known before
This blighted soul has lost his reason
Cast on the tide he sailed alone
But – there was light on the horizon
Light of the Lord, His grace sublime
Light from the Heavens, light of mine
Here in my heart I felt His mercy
This was the only course to take
Deep in my soul I knew His mercy
And this the only choice to make
And this, this course
The only choice to make!

*CAPTAIN DEE looks closer at STARLIGHT, who is still amazed*

CAPTAIN DEE
Friend, in your eyes I see compassion for this stranger
You're from the Watch, yet I have noted you before
Starlight they call you, yes? I know your kindly nature
Help him to find some shelter, I shall ask no more
Then I shall know no more
See there is cheese, there some old biscuits
These he can eat, see, all is free
Look at me now, a proper Christian
Take what you want, it's all on me!

*The MARINER wakes, looks blankly around*

CAPTAIN DEE
The man's awake
*(to the Mariner)* Friend, you'll be safe with her
Good luck
This girl will show the way from here
See how the Lord provideth shelter
Shines through a soul like me
Will find a man like me
For who am I? A humble sailor
No more to sail the seven seas
That's it for me
No more to sail the seven seas
That's it for me

*CAPTAIN DEE takes up the sack full of money, and hurries away to retirement*

*STARLIGHT gestures to the MARINER that she is offering him food. The MARINER shows that he cannot pay for it. STARLIGHT shows she's not asking for payment. The MARINER barely understands this kindness. He eats. Her movements are slow until she is quite still, frozen in his contemplation*

MARINER
Still is the earth now, light shines through the darkness
Where is the sail? And where the sea?
Whose are these eyes so gentle and so harmless?
Whose are these hands that care for me?
I who have sailed in loneliness forever
Long let me hold her now within my gaze
Unjudging soul, show pity to a stranger
So I might sleep in stillness all my days
But still they howl, those voices from the ocean
Why do you cry to me? I'm not your captain
Be silent, spare me! All I need is here
Home is the sailor, home from everywhere
Home is the world when there's an angel near

*STARLIGHT moves again, contemplating him*

**STARLIGHT**
And so he came, he is as I imagine
As if I dreamed him into life

**MARINER**
Still is the earth now
Light shines through the darkness
Gone is the sail
And gone the sea

He sits with me
Delivered from the ocean
Long has he suffered, now he's safe

Safe for a time but only till the morning
Kind are the eyes so gentle and so harmless    We must be gone by sunrise, disappear
Soon dawn will break, no mercy, only warning

Soft are the hands that care for me    Birds sing and there must be nobody here
Yet still they howl, those voices from the ocean    I hear her angry voice, she'll see I'm missing
Why do you cry to me? I'm not your captain    Oh, if they find you it's an island prison
Be silent, spare me! All I need is here    And all your life you'll be alone – I swear
Home is the sailor, home from everywhere    I'll save you from that place, we'll disappear

O, home for there's an angel near    Then we shall make our home an anywhere
For all I ever    Oh, if the Watchers find you here
Need is here
Then all your life you'll be alone, I swear
O, all I need is here    But I will save you from that last despair
My home, I see
Then we shall make our home an anywhere
An angel    Oh we
O home, when there's an angel near, my home
My home for all I need    Shall make the world our home
My anywhere!    Our anywhere!

Time all alone I knew forever
May all my time pass with another

*He goes aside, troubled*

40

MARINER
Still I can hear these voices of the ocean
Cries from the deep, I wished them all away
All else I knew is fading and forgotten
Still they pursue me to the brink of day
But they are dreams, they're only dreams
Will they not leave me be?

STARLIGHT
Soul, be at peace, whatever hell you passed through
You're here ashore in England, land of hopes
Soon you'll be free to lead the life you wish to
I'll help you find your way I'll guide your steps

MARINER
I cannot pay – see – what I had I gave him
Nothing but paper, still it made him smile

STARLIGHT
I need no payment! Love's what I believe in

MARINER
Love I remember… love that I can feel
Morning can wait for I wait forever
The isle of hopes has let me ashore
Lead me from here, my sentinel my saviour

The open arms I waited for!            STARLIGHT
The open arms                          Come, walk with me, we shall go free together
The open arms
                                       O broken one
I waited for
                                       I waited for

*STARLIGHT springs into action, taking a look outside, gathering supplies from the hut*
*The MARINER is once more tormented by the voices and visions in his mind*

MARINER
Ah no, they rise again, be silent
Creatures of night why do you weep?
Dawn soon will bless this holy island
Walk in the sun or forever sleep
I am of England, I don't know you
I walk free, angels guide my way
You are the cries of long ago, you
Cry the tears of yesterday
Only the tears of yesterday

STARLIGHT
Whom do you see where I see no one?
Turn from the past, all that is gone
Turn from your long despair on the ocean
All I can see is yet to come
Light on the shore, sweet bells are ringing
All whom we love are there, it seems
White lace and gold, speeches and singing
The world will know our names

MARINER
Bright town so far from any ocean

STARLIGHT
I see you strolling in the morning

Friends meet, and pass the time of day

I hear you singing with the choir

Green fields so wide

Here is a life lived in the sunshine
Golden hills upon the still horizon
Voices, O voices

Here lies the haven, heart's desire
O all will fade away

Hear me, O voices
Here journeys end
Hear me, O voices
Here journeys end at heart's desire
Here's where you fade away
Be still my soul
Here journeys end at heart's desire
My soul will know no ocean

Voices, O all will fade away
O voices, I beg you fade away

Whose are the voices
Still you're hearing
The faces you are seeing
Lay them to rest where all will sleep
Where all the souls will sleep
It's over now
It's over you were dreaming
Now you are free
And time is hope!

Cries from the ocean
Long forgotten

Lights of the evening, cool and low
The day is done
The sun is setting
Voices be gone
O spare me now!

## ACT THREE

*The SAILORS drinking, glad to be home*

SAILORS
Engaland Kingdom Come!
Engaland Down in One!
Home! Here! Dear! Dare
To be better than, greater than
Engaland Strong!
Forty weeks of hell our work is done
Made a golden ring right round our home
Now we'll dance and drink clear through to dawn
Better stay away from us or you'll be down in one
Storm fly away
We can see stars
Dream of a day
Make the day yours
Green and the grey
Marriages, cottages
Engaland, every man, ho!
Engaland safe and sound
Engaland home, home ground
Home! Here! Clear! Dear!
Engaland Fair
Dance with us!
Home! Here! Clear! Dear!
Engaland Fair
Engaland Here
Better than, brighter than,
Greater than, Engaland
Home! Here! Pure! Fair!
Dear come and dance with us!

*The SAILORS dance. They put the discarded cap of Captain Dee on HELM and pretend she's Captain now. She struts around. They ape her movements, even when she drunkenly stumbles. The WATCH comes*

WATCH
Hey, can't you see?
Look, there's a light
There's a light
There's someone there
But sailors, feel free, you dance away

SAILORS
Woah, cub-scouts, stop
What's up with you?

WATCH
Oh, don't mind us, we'll do your job
We saw a light shine there, it's gone now
But look you're dancing, dance away

HELM
Now wait! That boat, we know it's empty
We know, we know, our Captain told us so

SAILORS
No souls aboard

HELM
Not any more
No man, it's abandoned, look at it

WATCH *(to the boat)*
Hey! You there! Hey!
Your light, we saw
– Oh, could have sworn
How weird a thing

SAILORS
Dyb dyb dob!
Gold badge for you
Your work is done

WATCH *(to the boat)*
Hey! You there! Hey!
Show us a sign!

*Silence*

SAILORS
How sweet
Your friends have – gone to bed
They slept so well they woke up dead

WATCH *(to the boat)*
Hey wake up and show them we saw what we saw!
You shone us a light, you're no fun any more!

SAILORS
They're strong and silent, cool and blue
They'll make the perfect blokes for you

WATCH
Oh, drink with us, dead men, nothing to lose
Tell us what's new in the Afterlife News!

                                    SAILORS
                                    They can't be here, we can't see how
                                    They better pray they're dead by now

You've sailed all this way
Won't you dance on the sand?
Take a soft hand in your skeleton hand?

                                    They reached a world they'll never know
                                    So they can turn their bones and go

Hey neighbours, neighbours – anyone?

46

So brief was your light
So soon it's gone
Neighbours, neighbours
Anyone? Anyone?

*Silence*

Neighbours, neighbours
Anyone?

*Silence*

WATCH
There's no one, sure
So we were wrong
No soul's aboard
To hear our song

SAILORS
And why would there be
Any souls sailing here?
The sea has been swept
And the waters are clear

WATCH
We say they're scared
To hear you shout
You scream so hard
They won't come out

SAILORS
No stranger can make it
This close to the shore
Who sailed in their millions
Will sail never more

Hey
Losers
Losers, losers
Anyone? Anyone?

Losers, losers
Anyone?

WATCH
We heard of one
An engineer
He lost his wife
His girl so dear

SAILORS
Boo-hoo, very sad that
Let's search the whole world
For a stranger his strange wife
Their stranger dear girl

WATCH
We know it's wrong
It's wrong they try
It's just it's sad
It's made us cry

SAILORS
Hey phantoms, the cub-scouts
Have fallen for you
Why don't you stand up
Like dead men can do?

WATCH
There's nobody
So leave it be
No engineer
No family

SAILORS
Yeah brownies let them rest in peace
Rest in peace
We won't have corpses spoil our feast

WATCH
You ought to check this boat yourselves

HELM
Hey, should we tell the Captain first?

SAILORS *(mocking)*
'Hey, should we tell the Captain first?'

WATCH
Well so we came, we told what we saw
We'll take our leave, go dance some more
And if they're ghosts well then never mind
But if they're children treat them kind
No if they're animals treat them kind
Have a mind, have a mind, and be kind!

*The WATCH depart. The SAILORS have been waiting for this, they know a light shone from the boat*

SAILORS
Ha! Now it's their bedtime!
We saw that light ourselves!

HELM
We ought to wait and tell the Captain
We ought to sound the warning bells

SAILORS *(mockingly)*
Ding-a-ling-ding-dong
Ding-a-dong-dang-dang

*HELM flees the scene*

SAILORS *(to the boat)*
Let's have you, journey ends right here
We're sure you're all great engineers
What the fuck! What the fuck!
Out! What the fuck!
*COME ON!!!*

Time to go home, time's up!
Seventeen Wars, one Cup!
Home! Here! Dear! Dare
To be better than, greater than
Engaland Fair!
Come and take your tea and cake with us
Come and drive a taxi, ride a red bus
Come and live the life you dreamed about
Better still get out of here and stay the fuck out
Storm fly away
We can see stars
Dream of a day
Make the day yours
Green and the grey
Marriages, cottages
Engaland, every man, ho!
Engaland Rules the Wave
Thousands of miles, one grave
Home! Here! Clear! Pure
Engaland dear, dance with us!
Home! Here! Clear! Pure
Engaland clear! Engaland dear!
Marriages, cottages, villages, sausages
Home! Here! Clear! Pure!
Fair! come and dance with us!

*Suddenly we hear the TRAVELLERS*

TRAVELLERS
The cold sea, the lonely sea
We crossed the sea
Oh he and she and me
Oh, the air, we're here we're there
Sea shore
See the land
See the sand
Sea shore

Look upon
Little one
Sea shore
The journey ends
The life begins
Cap'n is gone and we're miles from home
Faraway faraway all alone
Travelling sheltering oh so long
Dreaming of anywhere we belong
Home is before
Home is the shore
Home is a family
Home is a memory
See the shore
Will the dawn
Never come?
Breathe the air
Are there friends
On the sands?
Oh, there is light
In the night like a home
Like our own in the mist, oh there!
You who can hear us then hear us now
Help us ashore for we don't know how
Travelling sheltering oh so long
Dreaming of anywhere we belong
Oh thee oh thee
Will you hear our cry?

SAILORS
What the heck, how the fuck
Make it stop, big it up
Call the Force, get the Guard
Go in full, go in hard
After three –
After me –
Let 'em see –

Engaland Rules the Wave!
Thousands of miles! One grave!

SAILORS
Home! Here! Clear! Dear
What the fuck –
Big it up –
From the top –
Engaland home, home ground
Engaland
Home!
Here!
Clear! Pure!

Time to go home
Time's up
Big it up!
From the top!
Come and take your tea and cake with us

After three!
Two three!
Engaland safe and sound

TRAVELLERS
Sea
Shore
See the land
See the sand

Sea
Shore
Look upon
Little one
Sea
Shore – will the dawn
Never come
Oh thee
Breathe the air

Are there friends

On the sands
Oh thee

TRAVELLERS
You who can hear us oh hear us now
Help us ashore for we don't know how
Travelling sheltering oh so long
Dreaming of anywhere we belong
Land of hope and cliffs so white
Woods so dark and window bright
Reach your hands towards the light
The cold sea, the lonely sea
Oh so far, so long
Oh so far, so long
Oh oh oh oh oh oh

*The SAILORS go to call the Guard*

*MARI leads STARLIGHT roughly to the shore*

MARI
What, am I dreaming? This I can't believe!
A nightmare? Starlight, is it true?

STARLIGHT
Why bring me here, I have no answer for your pain

MARI
He landed here, a stranger, he was seen
A man all dressed in black as in your dreams
What do you know? We heard them there!
Who do you know? How many more in there?
For this is treachery and yours alone
Miss *Starlight* ha!
Who sees for miles and miles
Who takes us all for fools, I know you now
I know – it kills me – someone came ashore
That man, he's in your eyes that slide away!

STARLIGHT
There's no one – lies – enough, enough –

MARI
Oh, but the story, *stranger lost at sea*
I'll miss this engineer who sails the ocean
Your heart his lighthouse, mine the littered shore

STARLIGHT
No more! No more! This man is in your mind
I have seen no one, I'll be gone from here –

MARI
You'll go nowhere, or not until we find him

53

What happened to your vow, your vow to the Nation?

STARLIGHT
What? Leave me be I'm nobody at all

MARI
Starlight, O Starlight, leave you be?
You I saw walking lonely through the evening?
You I saw gazing sadly out to sea?
You, I drew closer until I heard your breathing
You, I saw starlight when you turned to me
Remember how we walked and talked till morning
We thought alike, of holiness, of home
Old England's soul, its history, its yearning
Out came our stories till they told the same, oh
Ancient stories, how they passed the time
Precious stories till the day was gone
Then, we would watch, so many joined their hands
We stood as one, together through the night
High on the dear white cliffs beyond the sands
Oh, all the dark sea was helpless in our sight
Oh, all the sea was helpless in the face of light
High on the sacred cliffs beyond the white sands
Oh, all the sea, the dark was helpless
Hopeless in the face of light

*The MARINER rushes to the shore and sees his boat still out there*

MARINER
Abandoned! They're abandoned!
Oh I remember all!

MARI
I see him! No!

MARINER
See them, they live!

54

STARLIGHT *(to Mariner)*
Go back! They'll take you!

MARI *(to Starlight)*
What the hell now?

MARINER
They're mine! They're mine!
They breathe, they are abandoned!
They sail with me, they are no dream
Upon my soul they live and breathe!
They're mine, I
Am their only Captain

MARI
A plan now, I can see!

STARLIGHT
Go back!
The Guard will take them
You are free!

MARINER
I am theirs
I am theirs
Souls paid their way
And trusted me their Captain

|  | STARLIGHT | MARI |
|---|---|---|
| Souls paid their way | Surely you dream | The nightmare comes! |
| I am their Captain | Your soul is weary | Can I believe this? |
| Down through the years | This man is lost | I cannot hear |
| Over and over! | His mind is gone | Nor see, cannot believe! |
| So many lost |  |  |
| So many gone |  |  |
| Oh! Still I sailed | You're free, you're free | You planned it all |
| And still the night | You're free, to live the life | Starlight, oh |

The lonely night | You dream of | You betrayed the Nation
I am their Captain | Now I have saved you |
And they will suffer never more | | The Wave! The Wave!
They will be saved | You are free! | To shield the land we love!
I see it all | Now go, now go | The Wave! The Wave!
I see it all | Go! | To save the world I know!

*MARI summons THE WAVE from the Border Force*

No more, no more | My neighbour | To shield the land we love!
They shall not die | Go free | To save the world I know!

MARINER
You say I can be free?
You say you can be saved?
I will depart the man I was regardless
But this night at last I'll bear them to the shore
This soul-in-dreams has woken me to kindness

*[Starlight]*

Her light has kindled light in me to see
Those I have borne upon the waves
All the long night, abandoned here
I'll swim to them, the sea compels me
Darkness knows my name and calls it now
You cannot stand between us
One life is here! This light can grow
Do what you're doomed to
These will reach the shore through me
*(to Starlight)* Now – show the kindness
Shown to me I pray
The light that lights eternity

*The MARINER goes into the sea*

MARI
Oh swim then!
Drown then, let him go!

STARLIGHT
Now I can see
I see what has to be
What you will do I too am bound to do
Hand in hand our stories end
Foam white – the rags of gold –
Upon the endless shore

*STARLIGHT follows the MARINER into the sea*

MARI
No, no! The Wave is coming!　　　SAILORS
　　　　　　　　　　　　　　　　Yes it's coming!　　　　WATCH
　　　　　　　　　　　　　　　　God in Heaven!　　　　　Can you see it?
　　　　　　　　　　　　　　　　　　　　　　　　　　　　Heaven help them!

We can't stop it – no!

*THE WAVE appears on the sea, monstrous*

MARINER
Your Wave will come, O City by the sea
What you desire will come to pass now
But when your Wave dies on the cold and lonely shore
What you have made is lying in the shallows
The face is familiar, don't you think?

WATCH *(to the TRAVELLERS)*
Oh swim now, oh swim to me
Oh swim to me
And you and he and she and thee　MARI　　　　　　　　SAILORS
Ah you and she and he and she　　Starlight! Starlight!　　Drown him, drown him!
Oh you and thee and she　　　　　The Wave will come!　　Another one!
Yes!

57

*The TRAVELLERS are pulled alive from the sea by the WATCH and are 'clothed in gold' as Mari foresaw in her dream – in gold Mylar jackets; the bells 'pealing for the bride' are the harbour-bells sounding the emergency, as THE WAVE arrives, swallowing the ships, drowning the MARINER and STARLIGHT, and all is frozen in time*

STARLIGHT
Stranger and neighbour, we dream no dream
Sun rising – light – O sail us home